Welcome to

THE Feel Good COLORING BOOK

This book has been
lovingly colored in by:

_____

About this book

Firstly, thank you for purchasing The Feel Good Coloring Book – we hope it gives you many hours of pleasure and satisfaction!

The Images

The images presented here range from easy to medium difficulty, in order that you can best choose your strength according to your mood. The easy images allow for broader brush strokes and bolder color choices, which can be beneficial for a quick burst of 'coloring on the run' – for example; on the commute to work, or during a lunch break. The harder and more detailed images are for those times when you wish to immerse yourself in a few hours of coloring, and really get into the 'zone'
Each image features a positive, uplifting or motivating phrase, designed to give you a smile or a boost to your day. The phrases are all presented against a black background, set onto the floral coloring pattern. This is so that, when you have finished coloring the image, the phrase will stand out visually, and make a nice completed piece for you to display in your home, office, or surroundings.

The Paper

The paper used in the manufacture of this book is best suited to coloring with either pencils or with colored gel pens. Other media such as watercolor paints or pens are less suitable, and more prone to bleeding through the page. For this reason, each page is backed by a solid black page, to lessen any bleed through. Additionally, at the back of the book, we have included a couple of blank pages, which are intended to be ripped out for use as a backing underlay while you are coloring. If you wish to be able to remove any pages 'cleanly', we recomend purchasing a 'paper/page perforator', which will help. For those who wish to experiment with watercolor based pens or brushes, we have provided a link to our website, where you can download all the images as ready to print PDF files, in order that you can print onto white card, or watercolor paper etc. There is also the option to download a bonus pack of images for free!

The Fun

Finally, coloring is acknowledged to be one of the best therapeutic practices to relieve stress, calm the emotions, and focus the mind. Do not worry if some of your early efforts are not 'picture perfect' – it is the activity of coloring itself which actually benefits the mind and spirit. With 100 images to color here, and more available on our website, you will have plenty of opportunity to perfect your skills to the point where you can proudly display the results. Furthermore, when you have finished an image, and your proud of it, come over to our Facebook page (https://www.facebook.com/colourifica), and post your results – we would all be interested to see!

Above all else – MAKE IT FUN!

Color Testing Page

Use this page to test your colors. The boxes below have been placed side by side, in order that you can quickly see if one color looks ok against another.

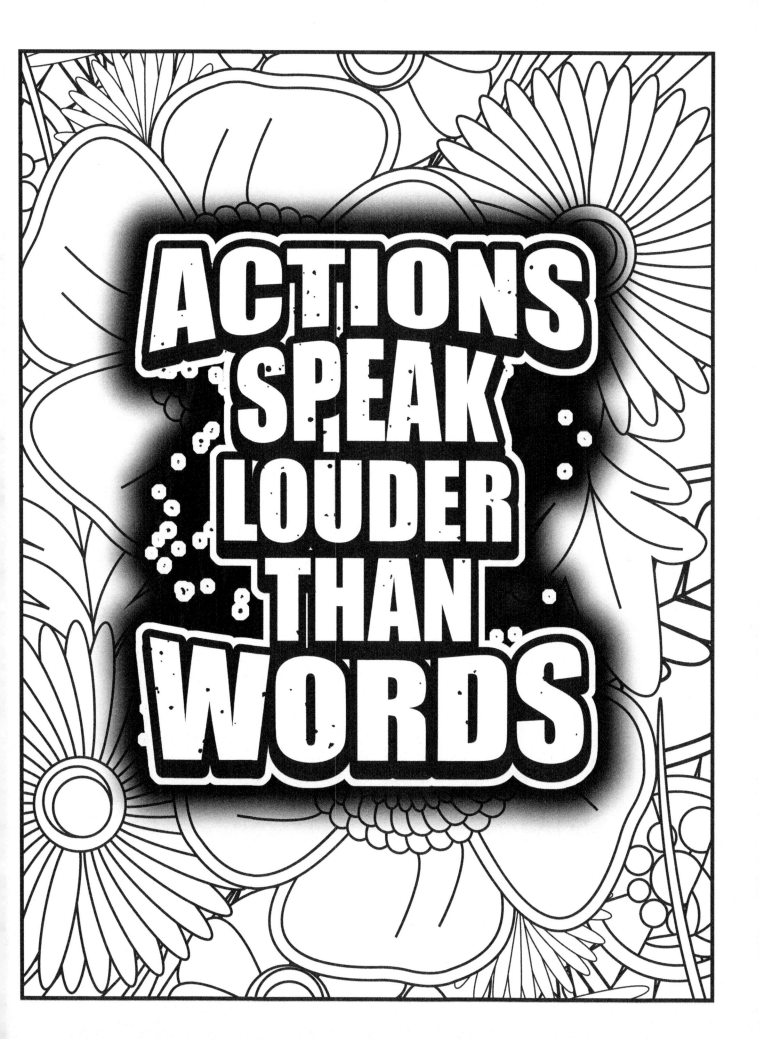

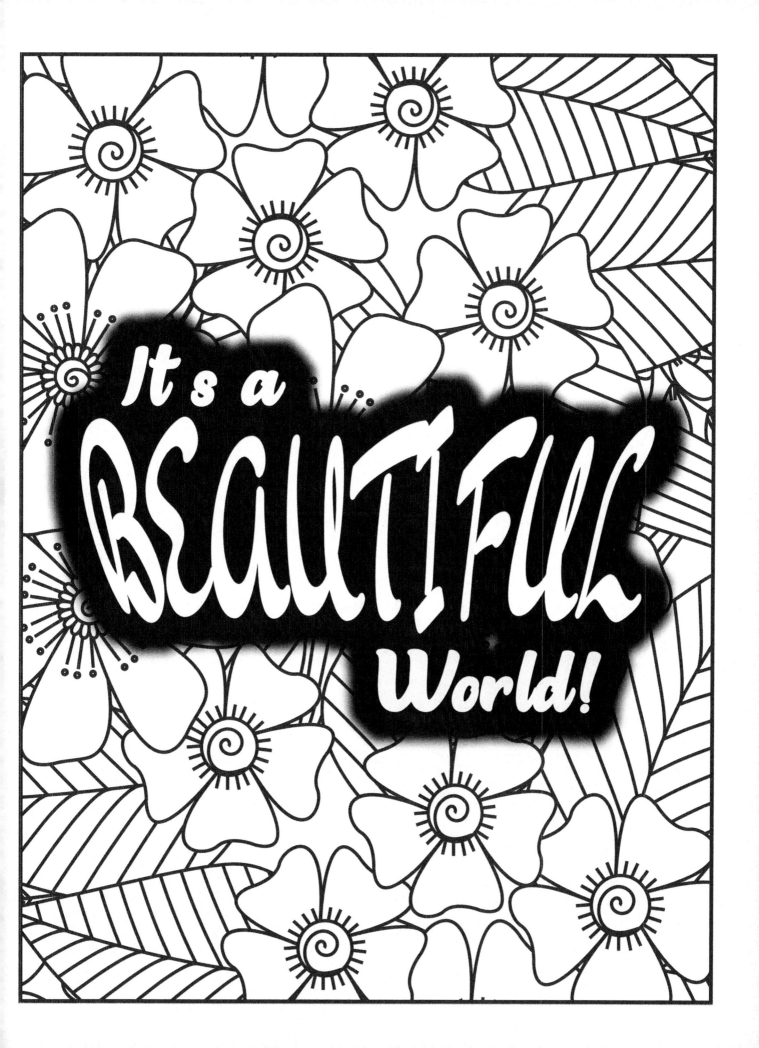

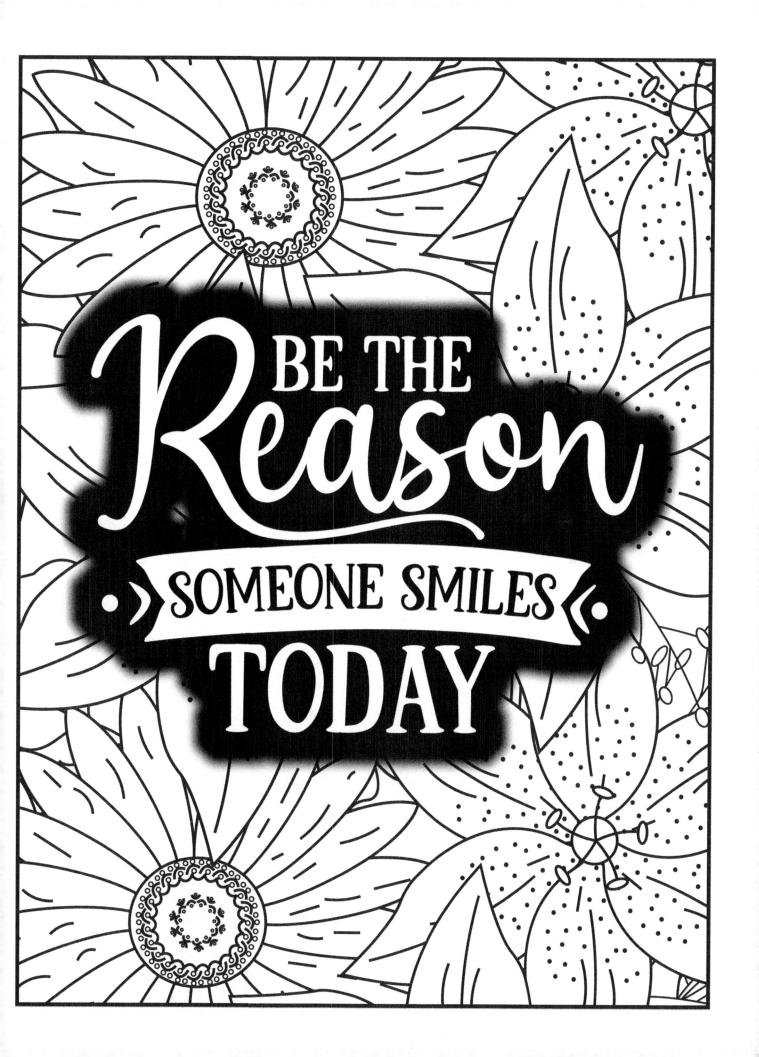

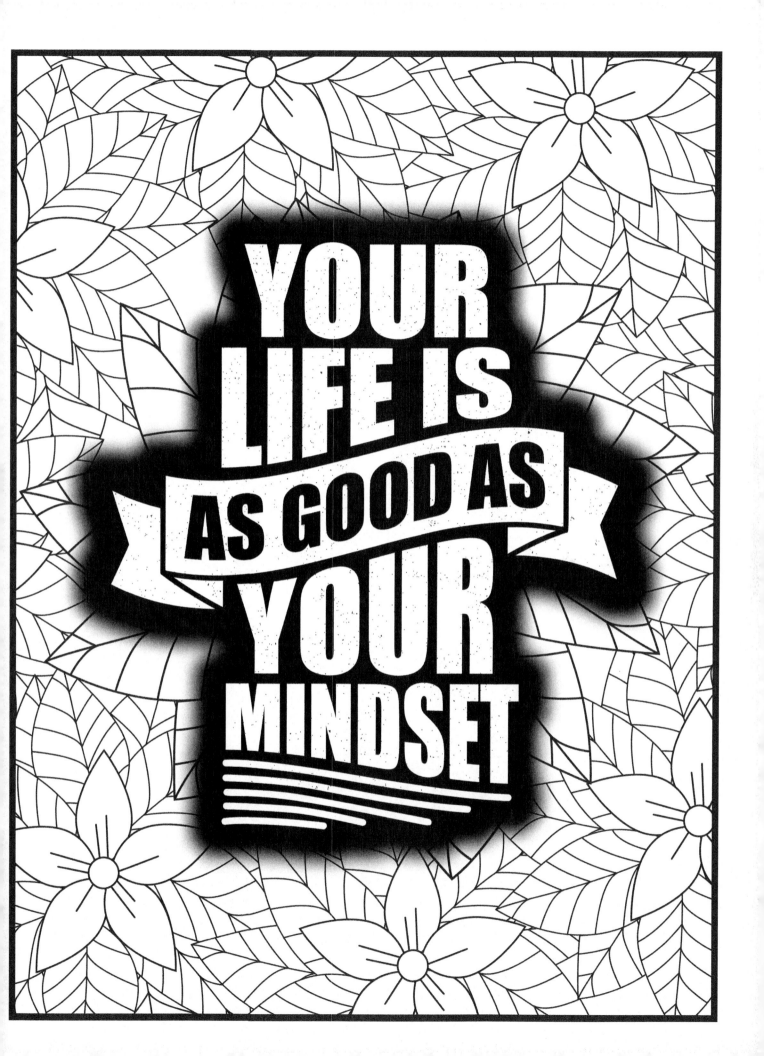

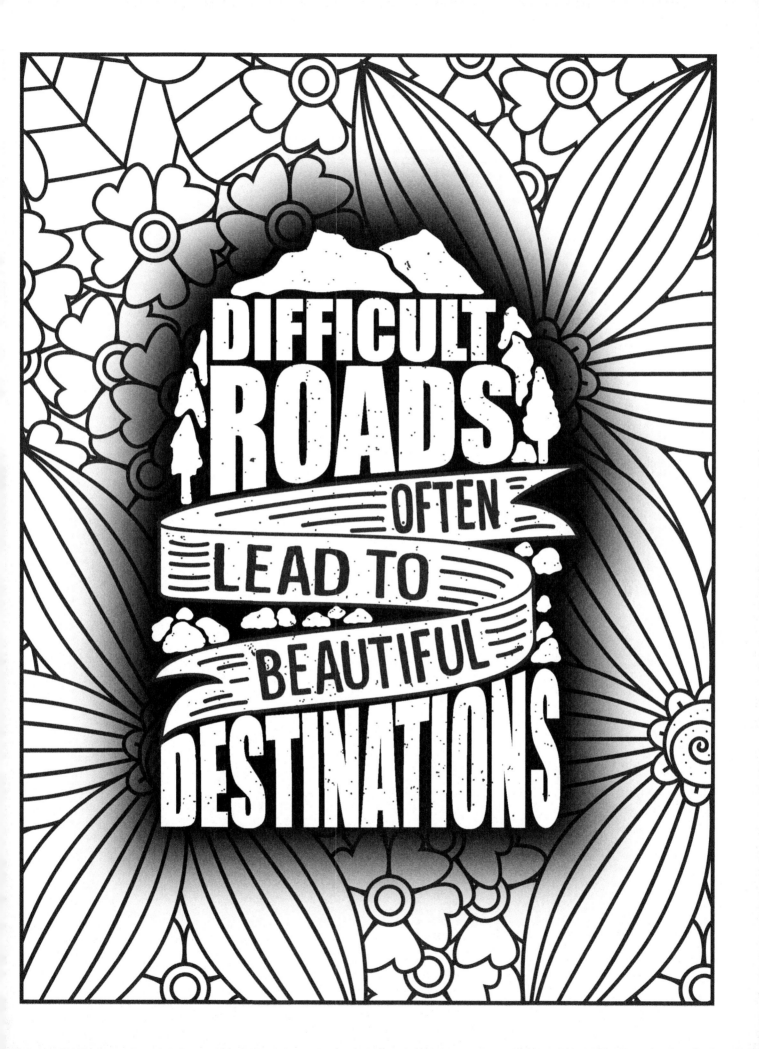

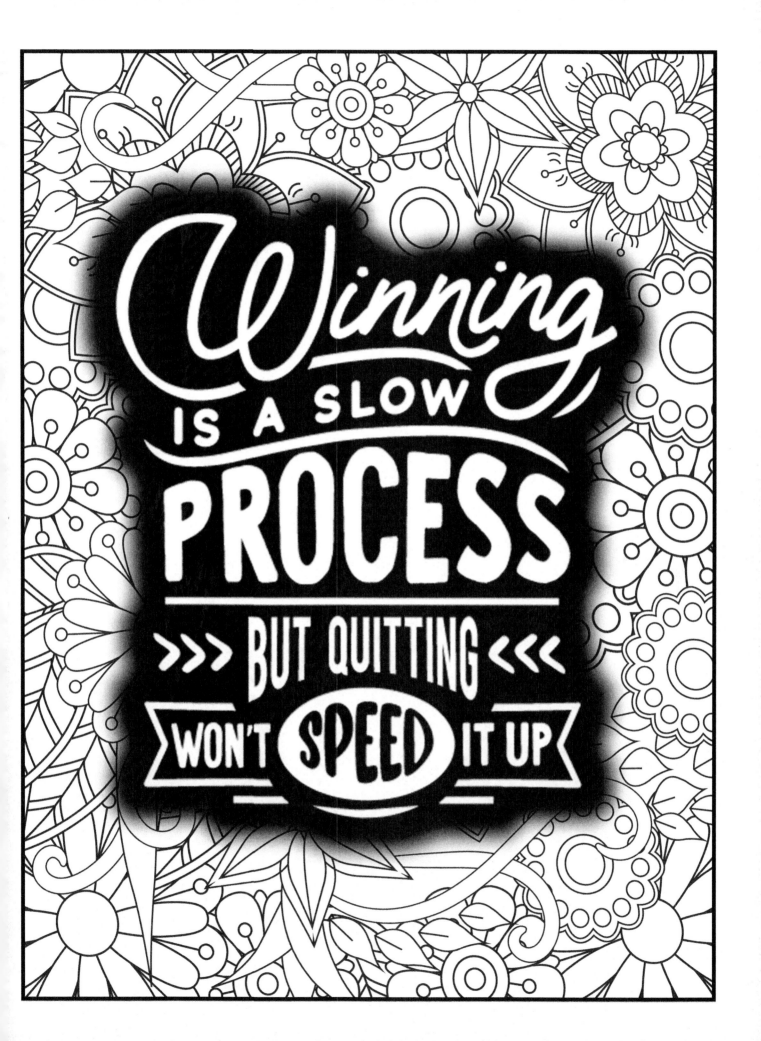

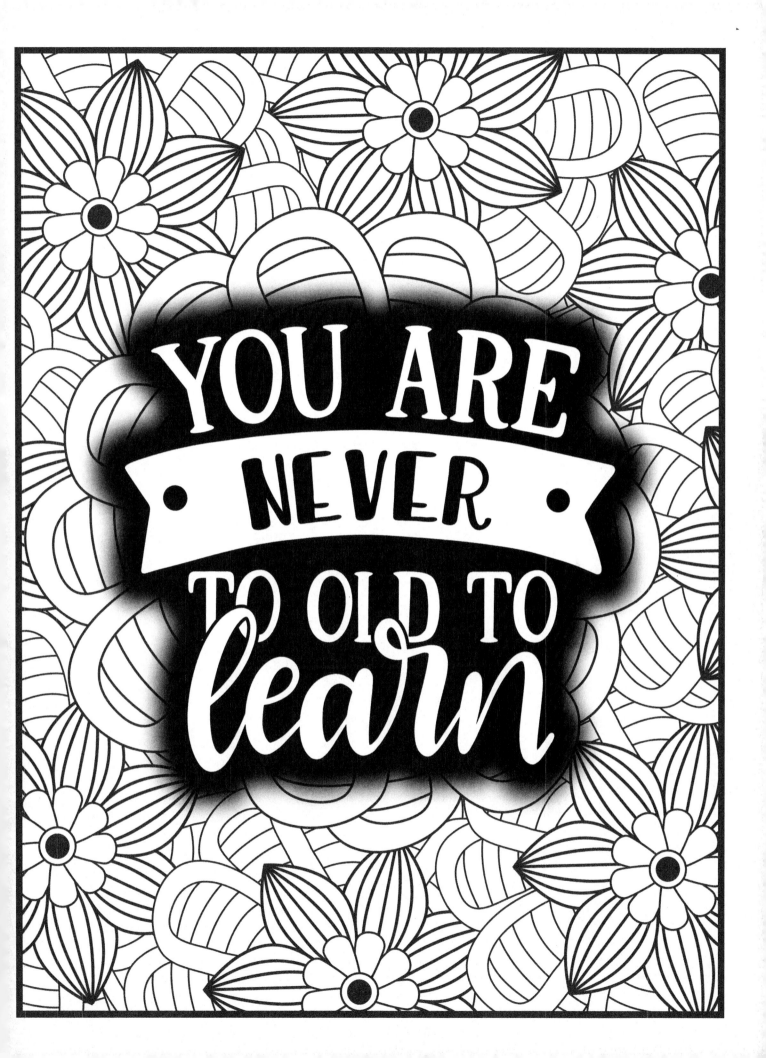

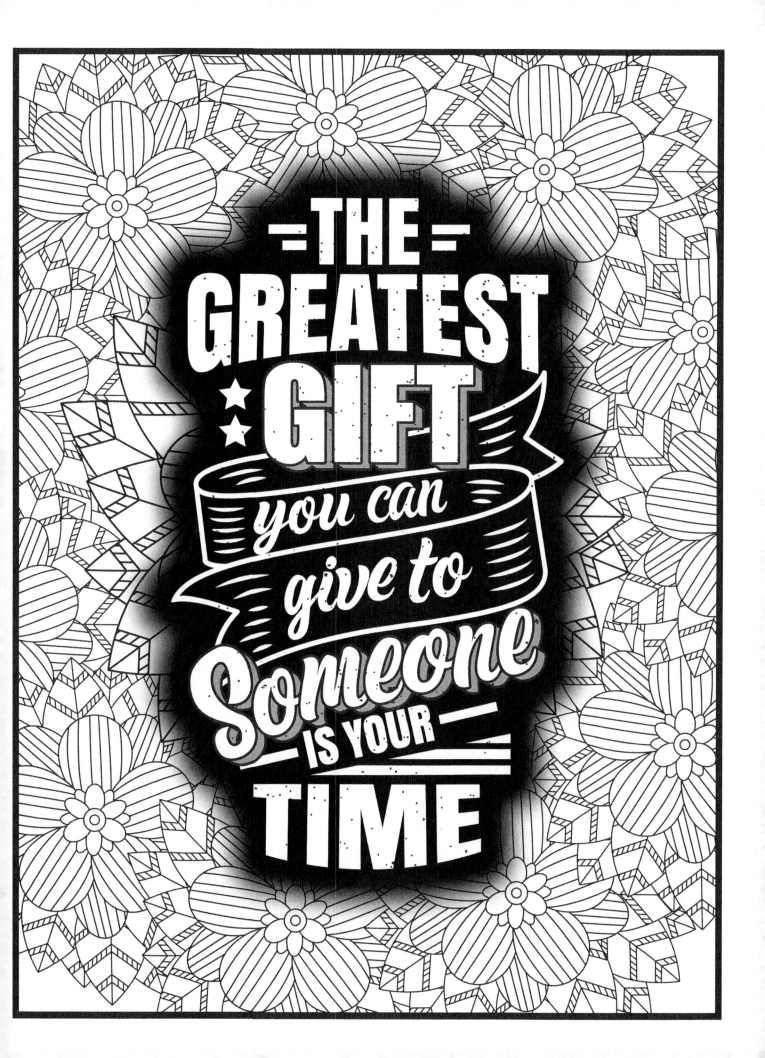

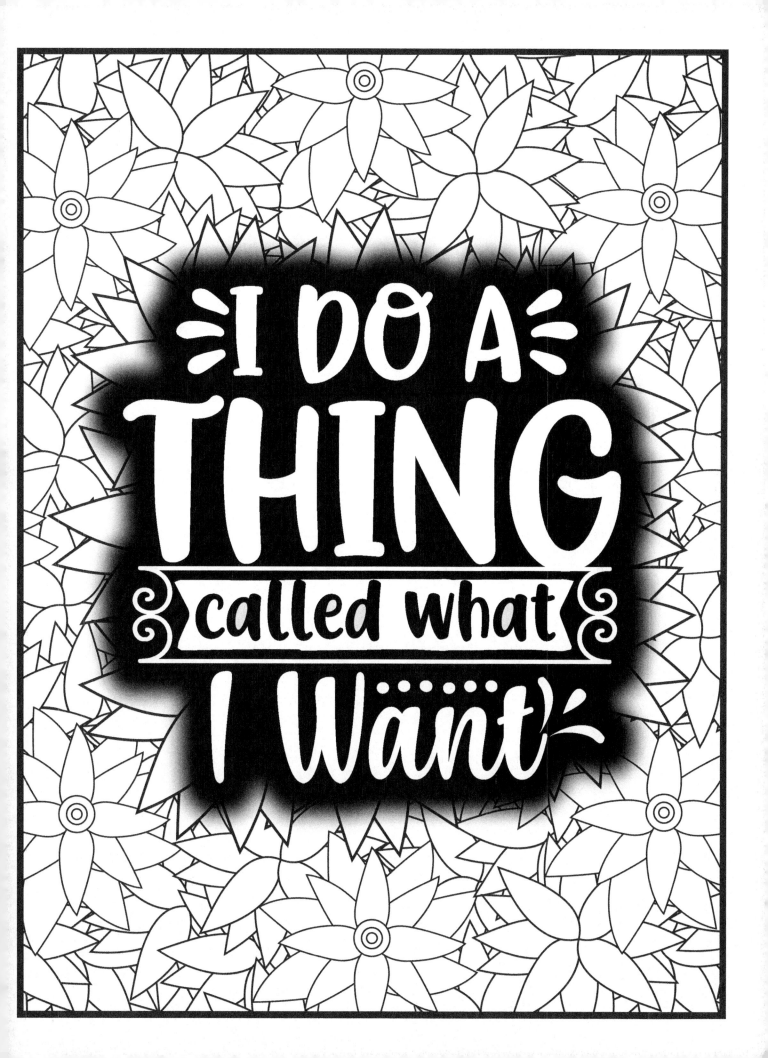

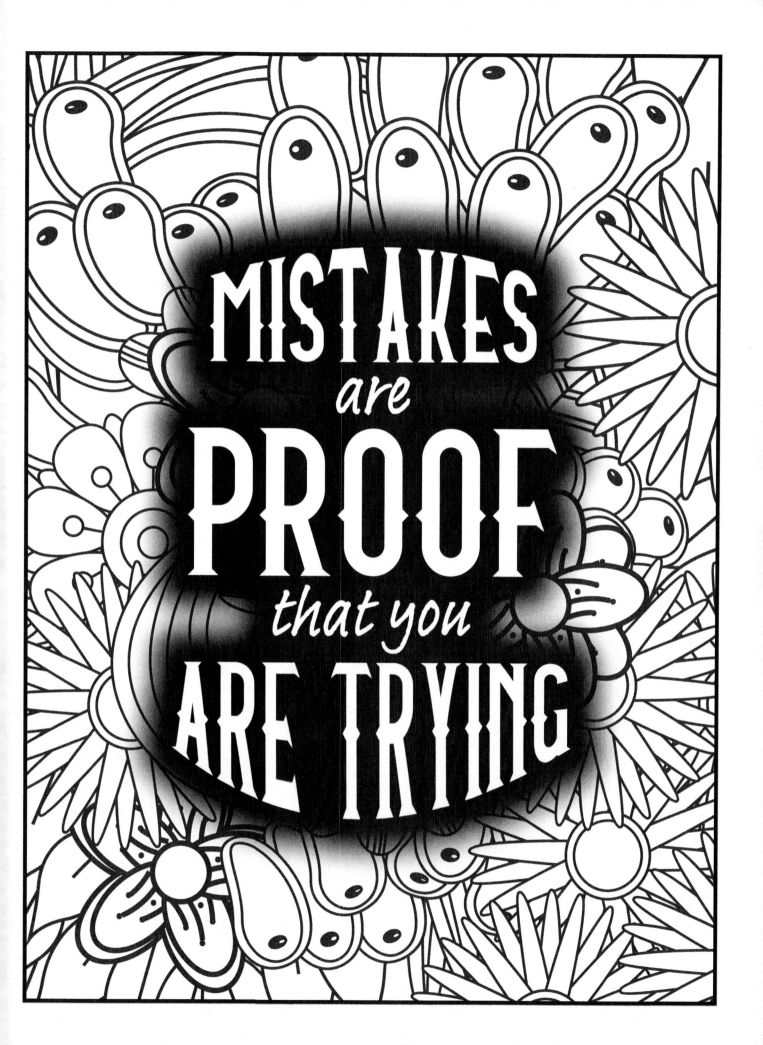

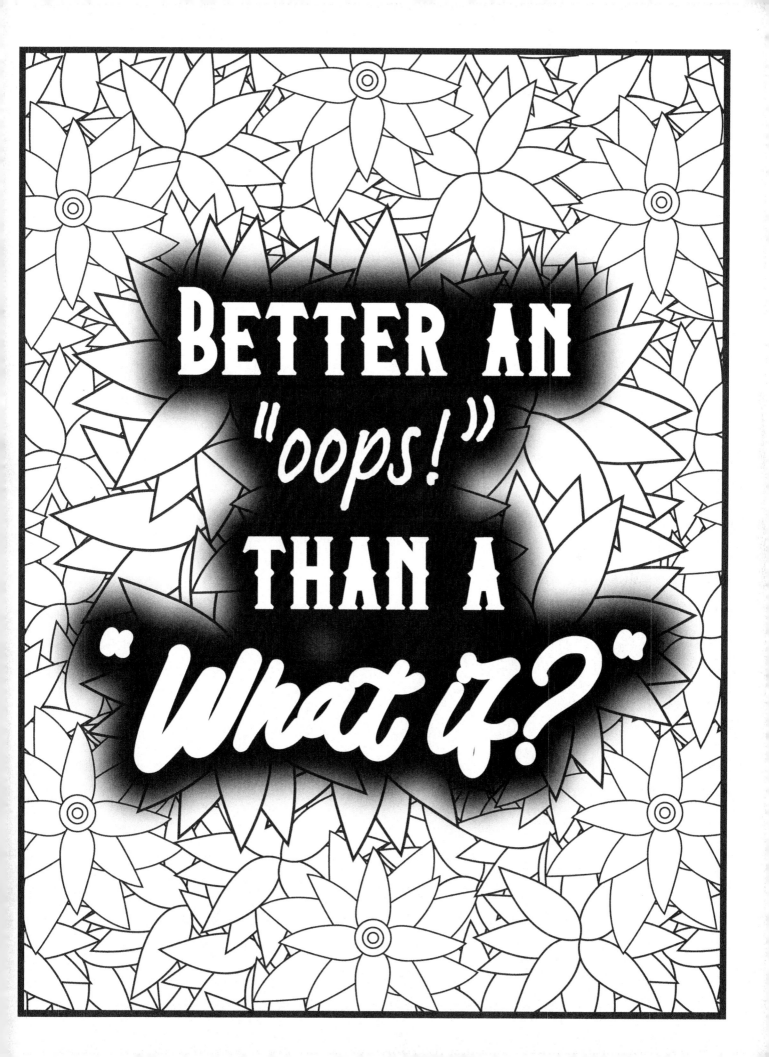

Thank You!

Thanks again for purchasing The Feel Good Coloring Book – we hope you are having fun coloring!

Please leave a review

When you have an availble moment, please head over to Amazon and leave an honest review. This really helps us to monitor what we are doing right or wrong for you, the artist. Colourifica is a new publisher, and this is our first publication, so we are very focussed on delivering as high quality a product as possible.

Free Bonus Images

Please feel free to visit our website: http://www.colourifica.com, where you can download all the images from this book as ready to print PDF files, in order that you can print onto white card, or watercolor paper etc. Additionally, there is also the option to download a bonus pack of images for free! See below:

Examples of your Free Images!

Finally, please head on over, say 'hi' and share your colored images on our Facebook page: https://www.facebook.com/colourifica

BLANK PAGE :
To be removed and used as backing page whilst you are coloring, to prevent bleed through

BLANK PAGE :
To be removed and used as backing page whilst you are coloring, to prevent bleed through

Printed in Great Britain
by Amazon

79499551R00122